American Symbols
AND THEIR Meanings

THE JEFFERSON MEMORIAL

American Symbols AND THEIR Meanings

THE ALAMO
THE AMERICAN FLAG
THE BALD EAGLE
THE CONFEDERATE FLAG
THE CONSTITUTION
THE DECLARATION OF INDEPENDENCE
ELLIS ISLAND
INDEPENDENCE HALL
THE JEFFERSON MEMORIAL
THE LIBERTY BELL
THE LINCOLN MEMORIAL
MOUNT RUSHMORE
THE NATIONAL ANTHEM
THE PLEDGE OF ALLEGIANCE
ROCK 'N' ROLL
THE STATUE OF LIBERTY
UNCLE SAM
VIETNAM VETERANS MEMORIAL
THE WASHINGTON MONUMENT
THE WHITE HOUSE

THE JEFFERSON MEMORIAL

JOSEPH FERRY

MASON CREST PUBLISHERS
PHILADELPHIA

First printing

1 3 5 7 9 8 6 4 2

Library of Congress Cataloging-in-Publication Data on file at the Library of Congress

ISBN 1-59084-034-8

Publisher's note: all quotations in this book come from original sources, and contain the spelling and grammatical inconsistencies of the original text.

American Symbols
AND THEIR Meanings

CONTENTS

THE IMPORTANCE OF AMERICAN SYMBOLS

Symbols are not merely ornaments to admire—they also tell us stories. If you look at one of them closely, you may want to find out why it was made and what it truly means. If you ask people who live in the society in which the symbol exists, you will learn some things. But by studying the people who created that symbol and the reasons why they made it, you will understand the deepest meanings of that symbol.

The United States owes its identity to great events in history, and the most remarkable American Symbols are rooted in these events. The struggle for independence from Great Britain gave America the Declaration of Independence, the Liberty Bell, the American flag, and other images of freedom. The War of 1812 gave the young country a song dedicated to the flag, "The Star-Spangled Banner," which became our national anthem. Nature gave the country its national animal, the bald eagle. These symbols established the identity of the new nation, and set it apart from the nations of the Old World.

To be emotionally moving, a symbol must strike people with a sense of power and unity. But it often takes a long time for a new symbol to be accepted by all the people, especially if there are older symbols that have gradually lost popularity. For example, the image of Uncle Sam has replaced Brother Jonathan, an earlier representation of the national will, while the Statue of Liberty has replaced Columbia, a woman who represented liberty to Americans in the early 19th century. Since then, Uncle Sam and the Statue of Liberty have endured and have become cherished icons of America.

Of all the symbols, the Statue of Liberty has perhaps the most curious story, for unlike other symbols, Americans did not create her. She was created by the French, who then gave her to America. Hence, she represented not what Americans thought of their country but rather what the French thought of America. It was many years before Americans decided to accept this French goddess of Liberty as a symbol for the United States and its special role among the nations: to spread freedom and enlighten the world.

This series of books is valuable because it presents the story of each of America's great symbols in a freshly written way and will contribute to the students' knowledge and awareness of them. It is to be hoped that this information will awaken an abiding interest in American history, as well as in the meanings of American symbols.

—*Barry Moreno,*
librarian and historian
Ellis Island/Statue of Liberty National Monument

The Jefferson Memorial is located on the National Mall, which is pictured here. The mall also features the Washington Monument, the Lincoln Memorial, the Smithsonian Castle and museums, Arlington House (home of Confederate General Robert E. Lee), the Franklin D. Roosevelt Memorial, and the Vietnam Veterans Memorial. The Jefferson Memorial is near the upper left in the photo.

A FITTING TRIBUTE

*I*magine what it would have been like to stroll through Washington, D.C. on a warm spring afternoon in the late 1920s. As you walk through the city you see the Washington Monument, a towering *obelisk* that stands as a symbol of our nation's independence. You stand in awe in front of the newly finished Lincoln *Memorial*, a symbol of unity and justice. You wander past the White House and the *Capitol* buildings, where laws and beliefs of this country are upheld.

And although you are impressed and inspired by what you have seen, there is a feeling that something very important is missing. Another memorial, perhaps a memorial that would honor a man who stood for freedom, equality, and growth, would put the perfect finishing touch on the area.

Maybe that is what Franklin Delano Roosevelt was feeling when he came to Washington, D.C., in 1928 as the Assistant Secretary of the Navy.

Roosevelt, who would become the country's 32nd president five years later, may have been disappointed that there was not a memorial dedicated to the memory and accomplishments of Thomas Jefferson. After all, Jefferson contributed a lot to the country's development. His legacy can still be seen and felt in all aspects of our lives. Roosevelt may have vowed at the time that he would do something to correct the injustice if given the chance.

It would take another 16 years for Roosevelt's disappointment to turn to delight.

In 1934, the United States Congress passed a *resolution* to establish a Thomas Jefferson Memorial Commission. The commission was given authority to plan, design, and build a memorial that would pay tribute to Jefferson's many accomplishments as president, politician, architect, naturalist, and educator. The commission's mission was to set a *foundation* for the memorial in the same way Jefferson's ideas set the foundation for this country.

However, before the commission could begin planning the memorial, its members had some very difficult questions to answer. Just how do you create a fitting tribute to a man who was so instrumental in the birth of this country? What type of design could embrace the spirit and essence that was Thomas Jefferson? Could it be done properly? If so, where should the memorial be constructed so that everyone could see it?

> How brilliant was Thomas Jefferson? When John F. Kennedy was president and entertaining a group of 49 Nobel Prize winners in 1961, he told the guests: " I think this is the most extraordinary collection of talent and human knowledge that has ever been gathered at the White House, with the possible exception of when Thomas Jefferson dined alone."

There were no easy answers for the commission. Early plans included displaying the Declaration of Independence, Jefferson's best-known piece of writing, in the National Archives building and placing a memorial directly across from the archives. Another suggestion involved creating a colonial-style library. This, it was hoped, would be a source of education and inspiration, so that future generations could follow in Jefferson's footsteps.

But the commission agreed with President Roosevelt that none of these plans were suitable for conveying Jefferson's high ideals and unique personality. Its members felt a proper memorial to Jefferson needed to convey all aspects of his character.

Eventually, the commission settled on a site that would complete plans for the National Mall, which had been proposed by the McMillan Commission in 1901. The McMillan Commission had planned to build a park with five points in the middle of the city. This had first been proposed by Pierre L'Enfant, the original designer of the *capital*. By 1922, work on the Washington Monument and Lincoln Memorial had been finished. It seemed only fitting to members of the Thomas Jefferson

John Russell Pope was an American architect whose most important design was the National Gallery of Art. It was completed in 1941 and since 1978 has been known as the West Building of the National Gallery in Washington, D.C.

Pope was born in New York in 1874 and studied architecture under William R. Ware at Columbia University. He graduated in 1894 and two years later began training at the American Academy in Rome and later at the Ecole des Beaux-Arts in Paris. He became a leading advocate of academic eclecticism, which is the duplication of historic architecture through painstaking study and research. This is what Pope did when he designed the Jefferson Memorial in the style of Jefferson's home, Monticello.

Because he was immensely popular as a designer, his services were in great demand. In addition to designing the Jefferson Memorial, Pope also designed memorials for Theodore Roosevelt in Washington, D.C., and New York City, and the Lincoln Memorial in Hodgenville, Kentucky.

Pope died in 1937.

Memorial Commission that their memorial would complete the final phase of the National Mall project.

Then, without holding a nationwide competition—as had been expected—the commission asked architect John Russell Pope to submit a design. This action drew considerable objections from many sources, especially the National Competitions Committee for Architecture, which felt the act went against everything Jefferson held dear. Essentially, they felt the commission's action was undemocratic.

The plan went forward, however. To Pope, the most fitting type of design was clear. The style would be one that Jefferson personally used for Monticello, his home in Charlottesville, Virginia, and for the buildings of the University of Virginia. It would be a circular domed design based on the Pantheon of Rome, which Jefferson believed to be a perfect model of a circular building. By using a design that had inspired Jefferson, Pope and the commission hoped the memorial would stand as a symbol of the very characteristics that Jefferson wanted for this country: equality, education, and *liberty*.

In 1936, Pope submitted his design to the commission. After considerable thought, the memorial plan was accepted. At last, a fitting tribute to Thomas Jefferson, one of our greatest founding fathers, would soon grace Washington, D.C.

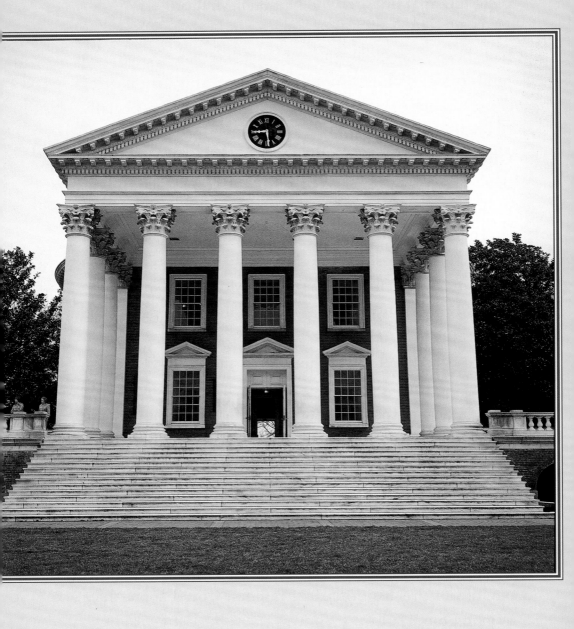

The rotunda of the University of Virginia was designed by Thomas Jefferson. At the time of the American Revolution, Jefferson was one of the most educated men in the American colonies. One of his proudest achievements was founding the University of Virginia, located in Charlottesville, in 1819.

A NOTABLE CAREER

Thomas Jefferson wished to be remembered for only three *notable* achievements in his public life. He had served a governor of Virginia, as United States minister to France, as secretary of state under George Washington, as vice president in the administration of John Adams and as president of the United States from 1801 to 1809. Yet he did not consider those to be his greatest accomplishments.

On his tombstone, which Jefferson designed and for which he wrote the inscription, there is no mention of these offices. Rather, it reads that Thomas Jefferson was "author of the Declaration of American Independence, of the Statute of Virginia for religious freedom, and Father of the University of Virginia" and, as he requested, not a word more.

Jefferson was born at Shadwell in what is now Albemarle County, Virginia, on April 13, 1743. He attended the College of William and Mary from 1760 until 1762, then studied law. In 1769 Jefferson began six years of service as a representative in the Virginia *House of Burgesses*. The following year he began building his home—Monticello—on land inherited from his father.

The mansion, which Jefferson designed, took years to complete, but part of it was ready to live in when he married Martha Wayles Skelton on Jan. 1, 1772. They had six children, two of whom survived into adulthood.

Elected to the Second *Continental Congress* in Philadelphia, Jefferson was appointed on June 11, 1776, to head a committee of five men in preparing the Declaration of Independence. He was its primary author, although Benjamin Franklin and John Adams both gave input on his first draft and the final document was changed in both style and content by Congress.

Writing the Declaration of Independence made Jefferson famous around the world. Years later John Adams was jealous of that fame. He complained that the declaration's ideas were "hackneyed." Jefferson agreed. He wrote of the declaration, "Neither aiming at original- ity of principle or sentiment, nor yet copied from any particular and previous writing, it was intended to be an

It took 40 years for Jefferson to complete Monticello, starting in 1769 when he was 25. It is now one of the most celebrated houses in the country. Its library contains more than 6,700 books.

expression of the American mind."

Jefferson returned to Virginia late in 1776 and served until 1779 in the House of *Delegates,* one of the two houses of the General Assembly of Virginia. Jefferson was instrumental in devising a major revision of the criminal code, although it was not enacted until 1796. His bill to create a free system of tax-supported elementary education for all except slaves was defeated, as were his bills to create a public library and to modernize the *curriculum* of the College of William and Mary.

In June 1779 Jefferson's bill on religious liberty was introduced. This touched off an eight-year-long dispute in Virginia. The bill was significant because no other state—in fact, no other nation—provided for complete

John Adams (left) and Benjamin Franklin helped Jefferson write the Declaration of Independence. However, Jefferson did most of the writing, and received most of the credit for creating the document.

religious liberty at that time. Jefferson's bill stated, "That all men shall be free to profess, and by argument to maintain, their opinions on matters of religion, and that the same shall in no wise diminish, enlarge, or affect their civil capacities."

Many Virginians regarded the bill as an attack upon Christianity. It did not pass until 1786 and only then through the perseverance of James Madison. Jefferson, by then in France, congratulated Madison, adding, "It is honorable for us to have produced the first legislature who had the courage to declare that the reason of man may be trusted with the formation of his own opinions."

In 1779, Jefferson was elected governor of Virginia. His political enemies criticized his performance as war governor mercilessly. They said he had not prepared to defend the city of Richmond in 1780–81, even though he knew the British were planning to invade. They also accused him of cowardice when he fled the capital during the moment of crisis.

In June 1781 Jefferson retired from the governorship. Afterward, the Virginia assembly voted that "an inquiry be made into the conduct of the executive of this state." Jefferson was *exonerated*; in fact, the assembly unanimously voted a resolution of appreciation of his conduct. The episode left Jefferson bitter, however, about the rewards of public service.

The death of his wife, on Sept. 6, 1782, added to Jefferson's troubles, but by the following year he was again seated in Congress. Jefferson proposed that slavery should be excluded from all of the American western territories after 1800. Although he was a slave owner, Jefferson believed that slavery was an evil that should not be permitted to spread. In 1784 the provision banning slavery was narrowly defeated. One representative was sick and confined to his room; had he been present, the vote would have been different.

"Thus," Jefferson later reflected, "we see the fate of millions unborn hanging on the tongue of one man, and heaven was silent in that awful moment."

For the next six years, Jefferson lived outside the United States. He was sent to Paris in 1784 to help negotiate commercial treaties. In 1785 he succeeded Benjamin Franklin as minister to France. Jefferson held this important post until 1789.

Thomas Jefferson held many important political offices in the early days of the United States. He served as secretary of state to George Washington; was vice president to John Adams; and was elected president of the United States in 1800.

THE POLITICIAN

On September 26, 1789, Congress confirmed Jefferson's appointment as secretary of state in the first administration of George Washington. Jefferson did not really want the job. He took it because Washington had asked. Jefferson was worried about the regal forms and ceremonies that marked the executive office, but his fears were tempered somewhat by his confidence in the character of the new president.

Jefferson began his duties as secretary of state in March 1790. He soon began to disagree with some of President Washington's other advisors. In particular, Jefferson did not get along with the secretary of the treasury, Alexander Hamilton. After Washington was elected to a second term, Jefferson resigned from the job on December 31, 1793.

The differences between Hamilton and Jefferson would eventually lead to the creation of political parties. Those who supported Jefferson's ideas became known as the Democratic-Republicans; Hamilton's supporters were called the Federalists.

Jefferson spent the next three years at Monticello, where he devoted himself to the farm and his family. He experimented with a new plow and other ingenious inventions, built a nail factory, started the rebuilding of Monticello, planted a thousand peach trees, received distinguished guests from abroad, and welcomed the visits of his grandchildren. But he also followed national and international developments with a mounting sense of foreboding. "From the moment of my retiring from the administration," he later wrote, "the Federalists got unchecked hold on General Washington."

Jefferson thought Washington's *expedition* to end the Whiskey Rebellion in 1794 was an unnecessary use of military force. When Washington spoke out against democratic societies that had formed to support the French Revolution, Jefferson was disappointed. He also considered Jay's Treaty (1794), an agreement with Great Britain, a "monument of folly and venality."

When Washington decided not to run for a third term in 1796, Jefferson became the presidential candidate of

Aaron Burr was born in Newark, New Jersey, on February 6, 1756. He was educated at the College of New Jersey (now known as Princeton), where his father had been president. Burr joined the Continental Army in 1775 and rose to the rank of lieutenant before retiring in 1779 because of poor health.

Burr soon earned a reputation as one of the top lawyers in New York City. He was appointed attorney general of New York in 1789 and served as a U.S. senator from 1791 until 1797.

Burr was a leader in the Democratic-Republican Party, a position that brought him into conflict with Federalist leader Alexander Hamilton. Burr ran with Jefferson on the Democratic-Republican ticket of 1800. Each received the same number of votes in the electoral college. To break the tie, the House of Representatives selected Jefferson as president.

Burr failed to win renomination as vice president in 1804. He also failed to win the governorship of New York, mostly because of opposition created by Hamilton. In 1804, Burr challenged Hamilton to a duel. They fought in Weehawken, New Jersey, on July 11. Hamilton was killed and Burr was discredited.

Burr later became involved in a plot to establish a separate republic in the Southwest. Jefferson had Burr arrested for treason. But after a six-month trial in Virginia, Burr was acquitted on September 1, 1807.

Burr died in New York, on September 14, 1836.

the Democratic-Republican Party. Under the system in effect at the time, a group of *electors* chosen by the states voted for the president and vice president. John Adams

As president, one of Jefferson's most important accomplishments was buying a large tract of western land from France in 1803. The next year, Jefferson sent an expedition to explore the new territory, led by Meriwether Lewis and William Clark; they are pictured here with their Native American guide Sacagawea.

narrowly defeated Jefferson, 71 votes to 68. Because Jefferson finished second he became the vice president.

In the presidential election of 1800, Jefferson received the same number of electoral college votes as Aaron Burr. As outlined in the U.S. *Constitution*, that left the House of Representatives with the task of choosing the president, and Jefferson became the choice.

As president, Jefferson looked to expand the young nation westward. In 1803 he completed the Louisiana Purchase, which added 800,000 square miles to the United States. He then sent an expedition west to explore this vast territory. Led by Meriwether Lewis and William Clark, the group found a route to the Pacific Ocean.

Jefferson's main concern in his second administration was foreign affairs, in which he experienced a notable failure. In the course of the Napoleonic wars, Britain and France repeatedly violated American sovereignty. Jefferson attempted to avoid a policy of either war or *appeasement* by the use of economic pressure.

The Embargo Act of 1807, which prohibited virtually all exports and most imports and was supplemented by enforcing legislation, was designed to force the British and French into recognizing American rights. Although it failed, it did rouse many northerners, who suffered economically, to a state of defiance of national authority. In 1809, shortly before he retired from the presidency, Jefferson signed an act repealing the embargo, which had been in effect for 15 months.

In the final 17 years of his life, Jefferson's major accomplishment was the founding in 1819 of the University of Virginia at Charlottesville. He conceived it, planned it, designed it, and supervised both its construction and the hiring of faculty.

The university was the last of three contributions by which Jefferson wished to be remembered; they make up a trilogy of interrelated causes: freedom from Britain, freedom of conscience, and freedom maintained through education.

On July 4, 1826, the 50th anniversary of the Declaration of Independence, Jefferson died at Monticello, where his body is buried.

The Thomas Jefferson Memorial occupies 2.5 acres in the National Mall. The distance to the top of the dome is more than 129 feet, and the dome is four feet thick. The memorial weighs in at a massive 32,000 tons. The statue of Jefferson is 19 feet tall and weighs 10,000 pounds. In 2001, it cost more than $1.6 million to operate and maintain the memorial.

THE
MEMORIAL

The planning and construction of the Thomas Jefferson Memorial provides quite a tale: the original architect died; several Japanese people chained themselves to cherry trees that were to be destroyed to make way for the memorial; and the statue of Jefferson did not arrive at the exhibit until four years after the monument was dedicated.

The memorial is a stunning classical structure that reminds people of the splendor of ancient Rome. Situated in East Potomac Park on the south side of the Tidal Basin, its surroundings are almost as beautiful as the monument itself. Jefferson was as passionate about

America's plants, birds, and animals as he was about the country's independence. He would have been delighted with the surroundings selected for the memorial in his honor. Plants and trees that grow in Virginia envelop the property. The capital city's most treasured natural specimens—flowering cherry trees—decorate the pathways that lead visitors to the memorial.

Franklin Delano Roosevelt was the 32nd president of the United States. He was elected for an unprecedented four terms (1933–1945). His New Deal program, which helped lift the country out of the Great Depression, used the federal government as a tool for social and economic change. In World War II, Roosevelt led the Allies to their victory over the Axis powers, Germany and Japan.

Born in Hyde Park, New York, in 1882, Roosevelt attended Harvard University and Columbia University Law School. He served as a member of the New York Senate and as assistant secretary of the Navy, a post he held during World War I.

In 1921, Roosevelt was stricken with poliomyelitis, which confined him to a wheelchair for much of the rest of his life. Despite his disability, Roosevelt continued with his political career and was elected governor of New York for two terms (1929–1933). In 1932, he defeated Herbert Hoover for the presidency.

Roosevelt died of a cerebral hemorrhage in Warm Springs, Georgia on April 12, 1945.

From the Jefferson Memorial, one has a clear view of the White House and the Washington Monument. It is situated in the National Mall, one of three national parks designed to be an ongoing tribute to American history. The others are the Washington Monument Grounds and West Potomac Park.

The design for the memorial was based on Jefferson's house, Monticello, and on his own drawings. Monticello was Jefferson's sanctuary from the world. It was built atop a 580-foot mountain in Charlottesville, Virginia. This was an unusual choice because it was so difficult to reach. But for Jefferson, it was the perfect location.

"I am as happy nowhere else and in no other society, and all my wishes end, where I hope my days will end, at Monticello," Jefferson wrote while in France following the American Revolution.

Preliminary work on Monticello began in 1768. Jefferson drew sketches of his vision for the house and prepared mechanical working drawings—a skill he had taught himself—for the craftsmen to follow. When it was completed almost 40 years later, Monticello was a grand two-story home whose central section contained a front hall, parlor, upstairs library, and a double-decked *portico*.

At Roosevelt's urging, Congress approved the Thomas Jefferson Memorial Commission on June 26, 1934. Nearly three years later, on February 18, 1937, the commission selected a location for the memorial.

Almost from the start, controversy engulfed the project. The memorial was not permitted to be a completely enclosed building because the Commission of Fine Art thought it would put the Jefferson Memorial in competition with the Lincoln Memorial. Architect John Russell Pope, who had been chosen to design the memorial, disagreed. But he finally gave in and opened the design of the memorial slightly.

However, Pope died in August 1937, while the project was still being prepared. Another dispute arose when his widow would not surrender the designs for the new memorial to the design crew. The commission took the issue to President Roosevelt and confusion ensued. The final memorial design was chosen in 1938, and the groundbreaking took place on December 15, 1938. President Roosevelt turned the first shovel of dirt. The structure's cornerstone was laid on November 15, 1939.

Another obstacle arose when the public became aware that thousands of cherry trees would have to be removed to make way for the memorial. Most of the trees had been given to the United States as a gift from the Japanese city of Tokyo in 1912. In protest of

> **The Cherry Blossom Festival occurs for two weeks in the spring every year. Band concerts, regattas, balls, banquets, and the largest parade in Washington, D.C., draw people from around the world. Individual blossoms on the cherry trees usually fade in three days but the overall display can last for two weeks if the weather is good.**

The Jefferson Memorial is visible through the branches of cherry trees in this springtime photograph. These trees were planted on the south side of the Tidal Basin during construction of the memorial.

the possible removal of some cherry trees for construction of the memorial, a group of women threatened to chain themselves to the trees. As a compromise, more cherry trees were planted along the south side of the Tidal Basin.

Still another complication occurred when Rudolph Evans was commissioned to create the statute of Jefferson for the memorial. Metal was being rationed during World War II, so the standing statue of Jefferson was cast in plaster, not bronze. After the end of World

War II, four years after the dedication, the statue was recast in metal and the plaster version moved permanently to the basement of the building.

The designers of the memorial based its look on the Pantheon, a Roman temple dedicated to all the gods. Its walls and dome are made of white Vermont marble reaching about 96 feet above the level of the walk that surrounds the building. The entrance steps, which rise from a plaza next to the Tidal Basin shore, are flanked by beautiful planted terraces. Carved in marble above the entranceway is a massive sculptured group, the work of Adolph A. Weiman, depicting Jefferson with four other members of the committee that drafted the Declaration

A sculpture in the Jefferson Memorial is modeled after this painting of Jefferson, Franklin, Adams, Roger Sherman, and Robert Livingstone presenting the Declaration of Independence to John Hancock.

of Independence: John Adams, Benjamin Franklin, Roger Sherman, and Robert Livingstone. The sculpture is modeled from a painting of the committee presenting the Continental Congress with the Declaration of Independence.

The memorial room, encircled by 16 massive columns of Vermont marble, is dominated by a heroic 19-foot, five-ton bronze statue of Jefferson sculpted by Evans and set on a six-foot pedestal of black Minnesota granite. It portrays him standing because it is meant to be a symbol of the Age of Enlightenment and because Evans wanted to portray Jefferson as looking out on the world. The statue is looking straight toward the White House. President Roosevelt said he hoped future presidents would gain inspiration from looking at Jefferson. The domed ceiling of Indiana limestone rises 67 feet above the head of the statue.

> The ceiling of the Jefferson Memorial is made out of Indiana limestone. The exterior walls and columns are made of Danby Imperial Marble brought in from Vermont. Interior wall panels are made of Georgian white marble. The ring around the base of the pedestal is Missouri gray marble.

On April 13, 1943, the 200th anniversary of Jefferson's birth, the memorial was dedicated. Its final cost was a little more than $3 million.

The statue of Jefferson stands in the center of the memorial. Around the statue are carved some of his most memorable words, including the quotation from the Declaration of Independence shown in the photograph.

WORDS OF JEFFERSON

To many people, Thomas Jefferson stands as a perfect American symbol of democracy and liberty. He believed strongly in the rights of individuals, government that receives its power from the people, the separation of church and state, and free and universal education. These beliefs became the foundation for our young and growing nation more than 200 years ago.

Although Jefferson was not the only philosopher of the American Revolution, his call for self-government established his reputation as the principle founder of American political thought. As the primary author of the Declaration of Independence, Jefferson managed to communicate the reasons why the colonists should be free of British rule. It took him 17 days to write and rewrite the document because he wanted to make sure every single word and sentence was exactly right. After he gave the finished draft to Congress, the members spent three more days going over it line by line. Jefferson was not happy as they changed a word here and a phrase there. But he suffered in silence as the final document took shape. It begins this way: "When in the course of human events, it becomes necessary for one people to dissolve the political bands which have connected them with another . . . they should declare the causes which impel them to the separation."

The Declaration of Independence is made up of five distinct parts: the introduction; the preamble; the body, which can be divided into two sections; and a conclusion. The introduction states that this document will explain why it is necessary for the American *colonies* to leave the British Empire. Having stated in the introduction that independence is unavoidable, even necessary, the preamble sets out principles that were already recognized to be "self-evident" by most 18th-century Englishmen. The first section of the body of the Declaration gives evidence of the "long train of abuses and usurpations" heaped upon the colonists by King George III. The second section of the body states

In 1999, 2,218,837 people visited the Jefferson Memorial.

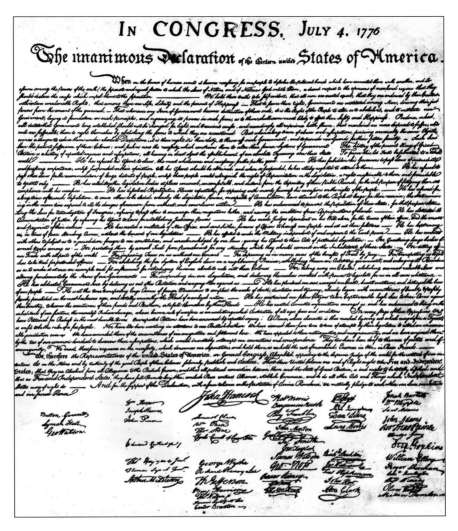

Thomas Jefferson's signature on the Declaration of Independence appears in the third column from the left, below John Hancock. Jefferson's is the eighth name down.

that the colonists had appealed in vain to their "British brethren" for a redress of their grievances. Having stated the conditions that made independence necessary and having shown that those conditions existed in British North America, the Declaration concludes that "these United Colonies are, and of Right ought to be Free and Independent States; that they are Absolved from all Allegiance to the British Crown, and that all political connection between them and the State of Great Britain, is and ought to be totally dissolved."

On July 4, 1776, Congress adopted the Declaration of Independence, at once the nation's most cherished symbol of liberty and Jefferson's most enduring monument. It listed the crimes of the British king and explained why Americans should fight for their freedom as independent states. It was one of the most important documents ever written in the United States.

To the founders, America was a great experiment, the first of its kind in history. To achieve the goal of free and

Visitors to Washington, D.C., stroll through the sculpture garden located behind the Jefferson Memorial.

stable government across a vast new land was to them a historic goal, a goal that would commence "A New Order of the Ages"—the motto adopted by the founders for the new nation.

The people who are part of that nation are responsible for a unique heritage. They have settled a vast and valuable land. They have, by their struggle in the Revolution and afterwards, secured liberty all across it. They have helped to defend liberty around the world, and they constitute what Abraham Lincoln called the "last best hope for mankind upon earth." By gaining and guarding their own liberty, the American people set a new standard of political principle and practice. This standard would provide unprecedented political blessings for the people of America. And it would shine a beacon around the world, calling for people everywhere to rise to the challenge of free government.

The statue of Jefferson in the memorial is surrounded by four walls on which are inscribed excerpts from his writing on democracy and the belief in a system of government that would allow citizens to govern themselves. On a circular band around the dome of the rotunda is inscribed one of his most famous quotations and one that seems to sum up Jefferson's philosophy neatly: "I

> The architects are said to have purposely misquoted and misspelled several words on the inscriptions that are included in the memorial (they claimed this was because of lack of space). There are believed to be 11 spelling or grammar mistakes.

have sworn upon the altar of God eternal hostility against every form of tyranny over the mind of man."

Etched into the marble walls surrounding the statue are other quotations chosen by the Thomas Jefferson Memorial Commission as being the most reflective of his thought. The first quote is from the Declaration of Independence:

> We hold these truths to be self evident: that all men are created equal, that they are endowed by the Creator with certain inalienable rights, among these are life, liberty, and the pursuit of happiness, that to secure these rights governments are instituted among men. We . . . solemnly publish and declare, that these colonies are and of right ought to be free and independent states . . . and for the support of this declaration, with a firm reliance on the protection of divine providence, we mutually pledge our lives, our fortunes, and our sacred honor.

The following quotes are also inscribed on the walls of the monument. They speak of the freedom that America is founded upon. Jefferson, of course, was a strong believer in independence and freedom.

> God who gave us life gave us liberty. Can the liberties of a nation be secure when we have removed a conviction that these liberties are a gift of God? . . . Indeed, I tremble for my country when I reflect that God is just, that his justice cannot sleep forever. . . . Nothing is more certainly written in the book of fate than that these people are to be free. Establish the law for educating the common people.
>
> —Taken from a letter to George Washington in 1786.

Almighty God hath created the mind free. All attempts to influence it by temporal punishment or burthens . . . are a departure from the plan of the Holy Author of our religion. . . . No man shall be compelled to frequent or support any religious worship or ministry or shall otherwise suffer on account of his religious opinion or belief, but all men shall be free to profess and by argument to maintain, their opinions in matters of religion.

—Taken from "A Bill for Establishing Religious Freedom" in 1777.

Still less it be proposed that our properties within our own territories shall be taxed or regulated by any power on earth but our own. The God who gave us life gave us liberty at the same time; the hand of force may destroy, but cannot disjoin them.

—Taken from *A Summary View of the Rights of British America.*

I am certainly not an advocate for frequent changes in laws and constitutions. But laws and institutions go hand in hand with the progress of the human mind . . . We might as well require a man to wear still the coat which fitted him when a boy . . . "

—Taken from a letter to Samuel Kercheval.

The whole commerce between master and slave is a perpetual exercise of the most boisterous passions, the most unremitting despotism on the one part, and degrading submissions on the other. Our children see this and learn to imitate it . . . "

—Taken from *Notes on the State of Virginia.*

1743 Thomas Jefferson is born on April 13 at Shadwell Plantation, Virginia.

1760 Jefferson enters College of William and Mary in Williamsburg, Virginia.

1768 Jefferson is elected to Virginia House of Burgesses.

1769 Jefferson begins building his home, Monticello.

1772 Jefferson marries Martha Wayles Skelton on Jan.1.

1776 Jefferson writes Declaration of Independence from June 11-28; on July 4, the Congress adopts the document.

1779 Jefferson serves as governor of Virginia.

1782 Martha Jefferson dies.

1781 Jefferson writes "Notes on the State of Virginia."

1785 Jefferson serves as special ambassador in France, a position he holds until 1789.

1790 Jefferson is appointed first secretary of state of the United States.

1796 Jefferson is elected vice president of the United States, serving with John Adams.

1800 After a tie vote in the electoral college, the House of Representatives elects Jefferson the third president of the United States.

1803 The United States completes the Louisiana Purchase, buying an enormous tract of land west of the Mississippi River from France for $15 million.

1804 Jefferson sends his personal secretary, Meriwether Lewis, along with Lewis's friend William Clark, to explore the Louisiana Purchase. With the 33-person Corps of Discovery, Lewis and Clark reach the Pacific Ocean in present-day Oregon, then return. Only one member of the party dies along the journey.

1809 Jefferson's second term as president ends, and he retires to Monticello.

1819 Jefferson begins working to establish the University of Virginia.

1826 Jefferson attends the opening of the University of Virginia; dies on July 4 at Monticello at age 83.

1934 Congress creates the Thomas Jefferson Memorial Commission, which is intended to plan and develop a monument to Jefferson.

1936 Architect John Russell Pope submits his plan for the Jefferson Memorial.

1938 President Franklin D. Roosevelt turns over the first shovelful of dirt as ground is broken for the Jefferson Memorial on December 15.

1939 The cornerstone of the memorial is laid on November 15.

1943 The Jefferson Memorial is dedicated on April 13, the 200th anniversary of Jefferson's birth. The final cost to build the monument is just over $3 million.

1998 The British science journal Nature publishes a DNA study by Dr. Eugene Foster, which indicates Thomas Jefferson may have had children with one of his slaves, Sally Hemings (also spelled Hemmings).

2000 The Thomas Jefferson Memorial Foundation issues a report concluding that Jefferson was the father of at least one of the children of Sally Hemings. The report is hotly disputed.

2001 More than 2.2 million people visit the Jefferson Memorial in Washington, D.C.

appeasement—to bring to a state of peace through concessions.

capital—city that serves as the official center of government for a state or nation.

Capitol—building in Washington where Congress passes laws and conducts other business.

colonies—areas controlled by a distant nation.

constitution—a set of principles that guide a particular group or nation.

Continental Congress—a group of men elected from all colonies to decide policies.

curriculum—a set of educational courses that include the knowledge necessary for specialization in an academic field.

delegate—a person who represents others at an official meeting.

elector—a person chosen by his or her state to vote for the president of the United States.

exonerate—to clear from accusation or blame.

expedition—a journey for a certain purpose.

foundation—the basis upon which something stands.

House of Burgesses—an elected group of men who made the laws in Virginia.

liberty—freedom.

memorial—something designed to help people remember a person or event in history.

notable—remarkable, distinguished or prominent.

obelisk—a shaft of stone that tapers at the peak.

portico—a covering at the front of a building.

resolution—a formal statement.

FURTHER READING

Adler, David. *Thomas Jefferson: Father of Our Democracy*. New York: Holiday House, 1997

Fisher, Leonard Everett. *Monticello*. New York: Holiday House, 1988.

Gordon-Reed, Annette. *Thomas Jefferson and Sally Hemmings: An American Controversy*. Charlottesville: University Press of Virginia, 1999.

Hoig, Stan. *A Capital for the Nation*. New York: Cobblehill Books, 1990.

Severance, John B. *Thomas Jefferson: Architect of Democracy*. New York: Clarion Books, 1998.

INTERNET RESOURCES

Information about Thomas Jefferson's life

http://library.thinkquest.org/17188/jefferson.htm
http://www.lcweb.loc.gov/exhibits/jefferson
http://www.pbs.org/jefferson
http://etext.virginia.edu/jefferson
http://www.theamericanpresidency.net

The National Park Service: Jefferson Memorial

http://www.nps.gov/thje/

The writings of Thomas Jefferson

http://memory.loc.gov/ammem/mtjhtml/mtjhome.html
http://etext.virginia.edu/jefferson/quotations

PICTURE CREDITS

page
3:      Hulton/Archive
8:      Corbis
12:     Bettmann/Corbis
14:     Art Resource, NY
17:     Art Resource, NY
18:     both photos courtesy
            Independence National
            Historical Park, Philadelphia
20:     Independence National Historical
            Park, Philadelphia

23:     Hulton/Archive
24:     Courtesy of the Montana
            Historical Society
26:     James P. Blair/Corbis
28:     Hulton/Archive
31:     Hulton/Archive
32:     Hulton/Archive
34:     Scott T. Smith/Corbis
37:     Hulton/Archive
38:     Adam Woolfitt/Corbis

Cover photos: Hulton/Archive; (inset) Independence National Historical Park,
Philadelphia; (back) Hulton/Archive

BARRY MORENO has been librarian and historian at the Ellis Island Immigration Museum and the Statue of Liberty National Monument since 1988. He is the author of *The Statue of Liberty Encyclopedia*, which was published by Simon and Schuster in October 2000. He is a native of Los Angeles, California. After graduation from California State University at Los Angeles, where he earned a degree in history, he joined the National Park Service as a seasonal park ranger at the Statue of Liberty; he eventually became the monument's librarian. In his spare time, Barry enjoys reading, writing, and studying foreign languages and grammar. His biography has been included in *Who's Who Among Hispanic Americans*, *The Directory of National Park Service Historians*, *Who's Who in America*, and *The Directory of American Scholars*.

JOSEPH FERRY is a veteran journalist who has written for several newspapers in Philadelphia and the surrounding suburbs. He lives in Sellersville, Pennsylvania, with his wife and three children. His other books in Mason Crest's AMERICAN SYMBOLS AND THEIR MEANINGS series are *The Vietnam Veterans Memorial, The National Anthem,* and *The American Flag.*